PURE DAUGHTER

PURE DAUGHTER

Poems by Debra Bruce

THE UNIVERSITY OF ARKANSAS PRESS
Fayetteville 1983

Designer: Patricia Douglas Crowder
Typeface: Linotron 202 Bembo
Typesetter: G & S Typesetters, Inc.

Some of these poems previously appeared in *Dissolves* (Burning Deck Press, 1977)

Acknowledgment is made to the following magazines and anthologies which first published some of these poems: "Medusa" and "Witches' Winter" first appeared in *Calyx, A Journal of Art and Literature by Women*, June, 1980 & 1983, *A Century in Two Decades: A Burning Deck Anthology, Cutbank, Field, Frontiers*, "Elegy for Clichés" first appeared in *The Georgia Review, Hanging Loose, The Iowa Review, The Literary Review, The Massachusetts Review, The Minnesota Review, Mississippi Review, The Ohio Review, Open Places, Poetry Now, Prairie Schooner, Selections, Seneca Review, Skyline, Southern Poetry Review*.

I would like to thank the National Endowment for the Arts for a grant that gave me time to finish this book.

LIBRARY OF CONGRESS CATALOGING-IN-PUBLICATION DATA

Bruce, Debra, 1951–
  Pure Daughter.

  I. Title.
PS3552.R7918P8 1983   811'.54   83-4811
ISBN 0-938626-21-3
ISBN 0-938626-22-1 (pbk.)

for my mother and father

"Immured the whole of Life
Within a magic Prison"

EMILY DICKINSON

Contents

PURE DAUGHTER

For My Sister

Maybe it's true about the wild
ponies at Chincoteague, how they swam
from a Spanish shipwreck through
the centuries. If you stand there
at just the right time in July
you might see their manes foaming
across the channel. You might not.
But it was already August, and you
were sixteen and disappointed. The marsh
was spiked with cranes sipping saltwater,
but that wasn't enough. If you couldn't
hear ponies thunder under the sea, you could
at least touch a lobster boat.
So we parked the car, and walked out
toward shore, but you flushed and stopped
when sailors hooted down
from the rigging.

You had a camera full of film—
The island shimmered with traffic
and there was nowhere to stop
but we stopped. It was hot, we were both
slipping in the weeds, and I had to watch you
patiently, furiously adjust the dials
and wait for a gull to fly just right
into your view, making the world really,
really perfect.

Hey Baby

Some men can strip
a woman down, while
they put a building up.
A whistle, a look—

One hoot from him as he dangles
from a moving crane, and off
go my clothes, and I am all ass,
ass, flaring with every step.
My body gets so hot so fast
it burns the air everywhere
with shapes of me but only he
can see them.

Chances are there's nothing hard
on him but his hat. Still,
what I feel makes my nipples burn,
and not with lust, or love.

Days

Along the cutting board, the afternoon grows
down to a spark, then glows around
these last few things from the garden. Soon,
from the porch step, I can hear the apples fall,
still sharp and green, pounding
in the wind. I wonder
where Bill is. I called
in every room, and the rooms
filled with the emptiest sound
I know. I've left the coffee on low.

I see him take the shears down
and wander to the edge of the yard,
run his hands
along the dry hedge, clipping there,
and there. September
on the screened porch. I remember
how we sat this time of year
feeling the cold light come on, before the boys went,
as it comes now, lengthening the lawn
to our tree where there are two green apples left, one.

Divorced Women

The bedroom mirrors reflect
from all angles that you've
trimmed down since him to the slim
size you used to be. Turning again,
you turn to yourself. The hip-hugging
fit fits, and dusky blue is the right
shadow for tonight.
Cosmetic kit, car keys, and the quarter moon
like a key-ring trinket. Your whole life
you've known only one man. Now
you will know how all men
are one, when their muscles melt
in motion, hips curve into waves.
But you won't drown. Just dry
your thighs and drive home, alone,
alive, with time for the first time
to notice how the September crepe myrtle
strips off its bark. Its petals
are so pink, too pink, and a late
summer storm has torn them up
and smeared them on the lawn
of your apartment complex.

Divorced Men

She was the best one
on the beach, but what a bitch
she was later. Summer after summer
she tossed, she twisted the sheets
on her side, she burnt the edges
of everything to spite you. The small
kitchen sweated grease, babies stuck
to her hip until they finally slipped
away from her and dropped, one
by one, into your arms in the backyard.
Like other fathers you knew, you
played ball with your boys
on a homemade diamond. You played
until your trick knee gave, until she
called through the screen for you
to bring them in. But it was just dusk,
you slapped your catcher's mitt
and shouted. You could still see the perfect
arc of your son's pitch, you thought
you could see everything.

The Photograph

Nothing changes.
The door to your room stands slightly open.
Through the years I can hear you
coughing in your sleep. The snow
breaks its crystals in a field.
A glass child, your daughter, lives
framed on your bureau.
Her smile is forming its mouth
in the dark.
The moon lights her cheeks up,
two white coins, then gold.

Athena

Motherless, out of pure mind,
say the books. My father
says nothing. But I remember
how I swam through his body looking
for light, how he forced me back

with his tongue. I stroked
harder, higher, my muscles dense
as a man's, my head aching
so hard, that helmet
was no miracle.

Such a long, gold
rain made him laugh
as one of his sons poured
down from nowhere.
Another of my brothers nested

against my father's thigh
until birth. But I earned my way
as Daddy's girl. I loved
the sour-eyed owl, I planted olives
in the pale heat.

Think of me as pure daughter—
carrying my father's buckler
and dangerous bolt.
Such heat would make anyone's
eyes flash. I feel it trickle

down my spine to a place I know
he'll never let me go.

Snowshoes

Floating is easy
with them, the netting
of my step hardly touches
the top of our white backyard.
All winter they hung
by the hunting rack, and smelled
of gun oil when I lowered them
in the dark garage. But soft,
and I strapped them on softly
and walk out now where snow
drifts into the woods,
and follow.

Nobody here, but the rasp
of the dried hydrangea
as I brush past, snow
scalloped with animal tracks,
blue inside. At dusk
I glide on soft piles
to the woods' edge, where overhead
Orion is stepping into
his field of cold dust,
the blade laid quietly
on his belt, the light
it threw down ten thousand
years ago just now
beginning to filter
into my father's field.

Crossing The Lawn

for Emily Dickinson

I don't think Heaven should be
so far that I can't see there
from my window, or walk
as I will today to pass
this nut loaf over the hedge to Susan.
I could slip out of the house
a summer morning, and lift
my hem along the damp grass
where even the lilies steam in sleep.
But to go now and not come back
would require I miss the garden
drying to gold this year.
Surely I would feel the slow
drowse of bees as I passed,
and pause. Or in November
the sudden light
of the witch hazel would sting me
into staying.
Or you, sir—
where you wait at the edge
of my father's yard, should I
look up too soon as I come
and see you look at me.

Purple Aster

Long nights nourish me,
inking the parched fields.
All summer I have withheld,
hoarding my colors
till they flooded the cells.
Now, in the August dusk,
deep armies of pigments
are rising in me.
Their chemistry stains me
with lust for my own growth.
Blindly, we are putting out
flowers.

Transplanted by the botanist
who observes my traits:
The pigment, he says,
is activated by long nights,
causing the aster to germinate
in late summer.

I say it's an aptitude
for dark.

Winter in Norfolk, Virginia

An instamatic flash of white
froze everything. Staring

won't make it thaw.
Such blankness takes forever and

forever to foam and soften and finally
drip one drop of ocean.

I must remember what navy recruiters
tell the boys up north

about warm, waiting ships,
off-duty beaches that ooze gold

bodies down to the shore.
They say winter only lasts

a few seconds here, then life
melts through. I hold my breath.

I feel my heartbeat through the crust.

Helen and Me

"All the powers on Earth cannot separate Helen and me."
Helen Keller's teacher, Anne Sullivan, before her brief marriage to
John Macy.

I don't know how
deep in her back or belly
she felt me coming across
the porch. One step
and her hands would stop
stroking words into each other,
and fall
into themselves, into her lap.

How could I punish her then?
Pretending I had seen nothing,
I let her nudge me, sniff
my hair. I tickled her neck
with whiskers of mimosa.
That summer she had already
kissed me back,
long before the word *water*
lolled in her cupped hand.

That year
I could hold her head
against my hip, and years later,
hip to hip, we walked
toward the hands of famous men
who touched her only
after I touched
their names into her palm
and let her go.

I've never known the long,
sharp shadow of a man
on a bedroom wall.

I know how wide my waist is
from her arms around me, the soft
shock of her breasts against
my own. I know how beautiful
she is, though her mirror
will never admit it.

How many times I've sat
there and brushed her hair
so hard it sparked, but still
she gazed from far away
in glass, and would not see me
sinking deeper in my own flesh
all these years.

I could tell him
I love him, but when I told her
I had to taste her
fingers in my mouth, and let them
follow my tongue to where
it scooped up words.
I had to learn
how strong the muscles
of my lips were, saying

please, yes, no.

Native Language

At sixteen I knew
what a tongue was for,
better than hands or hips
to get whatever
I wanted. My own father
and mother in love with it
would fall back and let me go.
I could funnel it
into any man's ear and leave him
dazed and lonely.

When I hear
your key in the lock
I feel something move inside me
deeper than deep
kisses, I go
for your mouth, your left cheek,
your warm, tense neck. I want
the smoke wet taste of you
in words.

I Haven't Been Able to Get Anything Done Since I Met You,

but I lie here anyway with a book propped
open on pillows where I stopped reading
when you started rubbing my feet.
In August we came in and spread
out this gold and orange quilt
of cats that your Grandmother stitched
for you, and sent from Czechoslovakia
to this room here where we let them roam
over us, under us. I remember the air
cooling on our skin, and one of us closing
the window one night, and I've slept every
night since with my hand on the fine blade
of your hip.
There's plenty of time to latch
up the storms before snow webs
our screens, before it gets so cold
we have to put our clothes on.
How slowly your grandmother must have stroked
these cats into place, for a grandson
she'd never see. She must have had in mind
that they would warm us this way, winding us
in their old, gold threads, their bellies
full of sun.

Elegy for Clichés

Remember how her face was like
a dried prune? But who ever thinks
of a tanned hand touching
warm plums, of sunlight
beating them until they sank
into their own skins
and shined and sweetened long
before they turned into grandmother cheeks.

In a story too pretty
to believe, I see your grandmother
run into the yard where a chicken hawk
just swooped. She scoops up one
of her biddies and sews its torn throat
with a silk thread.

Think of the silk worm spinning
a cloud of thread under
a mulberry leaf, of the smooth

skin just under your ear, of smooth
summer air on a soldier's face
in an Italian twilight we never knew
but my father remembers and insists
any young pilot would have wanted
to tumble through.

He rolled the B-25 just for fun
until the furious colonel called him
back to earth.

Think of a war that was over
before we were born, of time
flying, bombers flown by boys,
and the girl back home
who was nobody's mother
yet, by her bed a bunch of roses
gone sloppy in the heat,
her hair damp on her neck
as she brushed it down softly, violently.

For Bad Grandmother and Betty Bumhead

They lived with us forever
on weekends. But our grandmother's
blackberry cake couldn't fool us.
We knew a mother's mother was
a witch, and loved her mouth
to crumple when we took her teeth
from the bedroom jar and clamped them
under her rocker.
The winter night she went outside
in her apron, we followed and tripped
up her broom until she swatted us,
but she kept on sweeping snow
that kept on falling.

And who was Betty, mother's friend
who moved in with her smells and
no husband? The boys didn't care
but my sister and I slid under
the guest bed to see her undress.
So easy to judge, those grown ladies.
Small-waisted, she reached up to swab
her dark roots in the mirror, and we
squealed when the drugstore bottles
foamed and spit.

The closet ticks with loose hangers
as I turn to the bed
with these old cloth robes,
cloth buttons. My sister and I
fold them into my mother's boxes
and carry them out to the car.
There's dust on my fingers.
That year I would have blown it at her
and chased her back to the house.
But now we're just walking back, not looking
at one another, not holding hands.

Philomela's Tapestry

First I prick his eye,
sister. I watch it widen
with desire for me as it
watches me touch Father
for the last time.
There's home, a far off
corner of cloth where now
I cover Father with this
white robe.
Gray
for the long, wavy strands
that make me sick
of weaving, but you must see
the journey, the ship, I must
pull your husband toward me
again, snip his eyes into slits
as he fills us both
with lies. I am alive
near you. But see the knots
of green turn deep green turn black
as the forest between us, see
the thick, gold thread of his thighs push
against the cloth, against me
as I try to hold him back again,
again, until he is one bright
tangle in my lap and I must
force my own mouth open
for the final, purple stitch.

The Other Woman

Forsythia thrusts
against the screens and you're
back again. I haven't lost you
at all, you say, and prove it
with kisses with her taste
still on them as I slip
my tongue into your mouth
for the rapprochement.

Can't we be reasonable
about this, you want to know.
A gunshot of petals scatters
from the dogwood. Of course,
I want to know her. You suggest
she and I have coffee. Imagine
steam curling around the lips
of your two women. We could sip
your name together,
politely, and please you
that way.

But I want all
three of us to lie
in a room that sweats
spring rain. I want you
to trace her waist
with my fingers. Her hips,
you've told me, jut more sharply
than mine. Now show me.
You said the slopes to her
belly are steep, so let me go,
let me slide, slide
down them.

First Ticket

The cop's hips mean business
when they jut toward
my face before I can open
the door or say anything,
his whole body idling high
while I fumble for my license.
I already know his type—
22 or so, his fingers raw
since the winter he was 15
and hung out in back of school
and smoked. He'd drive breakneck
Saturday nights with Linda Lyons or
some girl crumpled
against his chest. He'd pull off
the road, cut into her mouth
with his tongue, and later
marry her. Now he loves
law and order, loves to catch
a blonde going 5 miles an hour too fast
for her own good. He slaps me
with a mean fine and I'm stunned
and watch him walk off just
like that, with one hand
riding his hip, one hand
smoothing his hair.

For the Boy Reading Playboy

On a page smooth as skin,
just as you flip her over
with your fingertip, I push
through the heavy door. Humid air
breathes into the bookstore, makes
you look up, blows her back
on her back again, and she looks
up at you.

Caught
by a woman, with another woman
in your hands,
you slip the August issue
under your arm, and wait
for me to leave. Excuse me.
You must hold her perfectly
flat against you while I wedge by
so close I can smell your neck.
Buttery hips could smear
all over you, even lips sweat.
But she is cool, covered
by darkness. Her body listens
for the slap of your belt
slipped off, the heavy buckle dropped.

I've taken boys like you
to bed before, and know how
the night cuts
shapes of women, pinned up
or pinned down. In the shadows,
drunk uncles would come back
from weddings to laugh and la, la, la
at us. And we would have to listen
all night to our parents, far away
in the stars, screaming
about something.

Fear of Love

At the edges of my body
stand the women you've loved:
One, her throat rinsed with snow,
says you left her that winter
in a country of marble.
Another, black-eyed,
says the olive groves still blaze toward Florence
at dawn. In that valley of blue slopes
she remembers how you explained
Botticelli's *Birth of Venus*.
In her quilted robe, your mother
is inviting you home for Thanksgiving.
In the doorway of a house
I've never seen, she waits
to fold you back into her.

If I could say
I can't imagine life with you
if I could grieve
as the planets clog nightly
in the birch tree,
but I can't

and already
the white lawns of our deaths
stretch out, where our children
keep putting on their hoods.

The Storm

In my father's house. . .
a plate full of chicken bones
and a wide-eyed arch
opening the hallway.
I remember before the house caved in—
cushions of gingerbread
and a bicycle in the rain,
two brothers pushing its wet frame
through the back door,
the whining of spokes and chains.

The summer the house fell
in a storm of voices,
the winds were out of my father,
then slow rains
were the crying of my father
over the chicken plates
or over the broken back step
or the bare apple tree.

The summer the house fell
its walls lay down,
breathing like tired men.
The curtains whispered,
then folded their flowery ears.
The china splashed.

It was a storm of glass,
of broken colors.
My father's eyes were splintered
and bled with crystal.

Only the cat could see—
tightening its claws
on a tall, backyard birch
with the gold spoons of its eyes saying
      The house is falling
      The house is falling
with the gold flash from its eyes
warning the tree.

Perspective

Actually snowing at this moment! . . . the folly of people not staying comfortably at home when they can.
Emma Jane Austen

Horses steam with frost
as the groom tethers them.
The first flakes slow
the carriage, and no one looks
at roads going wild with white.
No one breathes until they're
safely by the fire. Winters
in this novel, young women
fold their tippets and stay
inside with their fathers.

In another world we stay inside
and watch the radar weatherscope.
Years flash their record lows
on the screen, and in the satellite photo
we see ghostly clouds grazing
our map in April with snow.

We won't remember what we said
tonight, or how we lived here,
hardly touching. Snow touches
everywhere, the crocus that opened
by the porch of this house,
the separate porches where we'll stand
looking back on a spring so white
we can't see anything.

At the Drive-In

Our summer rides took us
past the ticket booth,
on the road curving around
the fence. The ferns lay
back where my father parked.
We watched other drivers pay
and file with their families
over gravel. The theatre air
was smoky with dusk, the screen
lit up. Where the fence broke
my father crept through, wired
the voices to our car,
lifted us high on the roof
for the best view.

Driving on any dusky
loop of road, I turn
to see the actors' lives
go by. Four children
and a father climbed up
for a free show. The roof
of the car is still warm
where they looked from
one world, into another.

Blue Mountain

for my father

You never finished your story
that day, about your first ride
at dawn on the milk truck.
You were fourteen then, wearing
a man's gloves, setting the tinkling
bottles down, stoop after stoop.
The blue film on the mountain lifted
and the town woke while you worked.
While we listened, Grandma's gray,
plaited hair washed back into blonde
and unwound from her comb. We saw her
still waiting for you, on the wicker chair,
in the kitchen.

But your old house was boarded
and the tall grass crouched
when we drove up. You were
thinking of something else now,
that shack in back of the house,
deer season. For years you used to
come back, oil your rifle and go
into these woods. The shack was sealed up
where you and Jimmy Johnson stayed
for almost nothing.

It was getting late. The town
was cooling in August.
My sister and I
kept up with you into the field,
carrying the camera. The sun burnt low
on the mountain, around it like
blue smoke. In the photograph
you shade your eyes and look back
from where the goldenrod grows.

That fall I leaned the mountain
on my mantel, against the wall.
You stand there in summer, all these winters.
Blue steams, goldenrod
keeps filling up the frame.
What are you looking for?

Epistemology

The foam of the apple
on your tongue
is the beginning:

You know
how your cells ingest,
sucking through their skins,
how the inner pods
store the life of the apple
in hot crystals.
Certain parts of you
repeat themselves:
The cell, in love with its image,
divides.
Ladders of mirrors
clutch their own rungs.
Certain parts
die hourly:
The outer gold of your wrist
scales off.
The lights of inner walls
drench themselves in darkness
each month.

You brush your hair in the mirror.
You feel the same.

Our Lady of Angels' Sight Saving Class

Whatever you can't see
God will let you get closer
in this class.
In Kathy's braille reader, Puff's
raised fur touches her fingers
when she finds him, while I see
Puff as a cloud of gold
in the large type edition,
and I follow tall words that tell me
the friendly policeman Bill is bringing
the lost cat home.
How dark is it, I want Kathy
to tell me. I squeeze my eyes
shut but light still sizzles
under the lids. No, she says
she can't see dark, she can't see
anything. At noon Sister Anna
lets us go after we pray
and promise to hold hands.

At home
I'm like the others but
I sit closer to watch TV.
My mother tells me to move back
but I'm not afraid to stare
at the jumpy light, to stare
straight at darkness in my bedroom
until I finally break it
into static, dust, stars.
Some children see everything
this way, their own hands
are shadows, Sister Anna's habit
grazes their desks like a cloud.
They will never watch

from their beds and see how
bedroom furniture falls
into place at night,
how the painting of Jesus
is a darker and darker square
over there, on the wall
where he's watching all
of us, everywhere, all the time.

Dr. Martin's Day Off

His legs loosen easily
into the morning run, a half-mile
to the docks where small boats
rock themselves and mallards squabble
like crones, a half-mile back.
He's far from his clinic
where the girls are getting younger
every summer as they breeze through.
He lets the nurses tell them
how to stop it from happening
again, with a pill, a loop, a cup.
Some, at twenty, are already drugged
from babies' mouths. Some
are sixteen and did it just
to taste a boy, and that's
how it all began.

They lie on his table, their mouths
ripening into pouts as they breathe in,
breathe out, letting go
of the six-week one-sixth of an inch
of flesh that even his fibroscopic photos
prove is nothing.

Always more girls, all day,
all week, so thank God
for nice weather when he's finally free.
He can read his medical journals
on the patio. He can smell honeysuckle
a whole block away, and see the yards full
of pink and red petals where the camellias
have come and gone, come
and gone without him.

The Arrangement

Tuesday nights are hers
with her lover, and since
possession is wrong, her husband
agrees to share. So he gets

the cats and kitchen clocks
and the thought of her, last night,
sipping herbal tea. After he eats,
he lets the lips of strange women

flap open in his magazines.
Thinking of her with another man
is a turn-on. The brain's our best
sex organ, and the brain's painless, so

what hurts? Nothing on TV, nothing
outside but lightning bugs.
One bolt of bright juice
through their bodies, and they fly

through the quiet neighborhood.
9 o'clock. The sky steams as usual,
and he knows how sweat pours hard
down the backs of boys tonight,

how they'll slip
into their girls, and against
good sense, promise to stay
forever, and ever, and ever.

Brief

1

The husband and wife park
their cars below a marble dome.
December air files them
through the courthouse doors
so early, the lawyers' hands
are still slack, and warm.
But at 9:00 their briefcases
snap open.

2

Summer nights, he watched
for her headlights on the lawn.
They swung past him and he
heard her shopping bags crumple
in the dark, the screen-door
slam. He took his flashlight
and wandered out back
making small circles of light.

3

A woman can't sleep.
She smooths the sheets back
and looks out at snow.
She knots her robe at the waist,
and waits. The man on the porch
is drunk. He slides to his knees.
A father sleeps that way, hunched
outside in his hunting jacket.
A mother walks all night from
room to room of their house,
locking each door.

4
The lawyers clip the list,
what's hers, what's his.
2 picnic tables, 2 cars.
They don't know that one summer
he drove back from the Adirondacks
with a carful of small trees
and nudged them into the earth,
laughing, *One for each daughter.*

5
In winter whoever lives here
will plow. But he comes back,
wading through snowdrifts
at dawn. When Mrs. Silva turns
her light on she sees the man
next door staring at his house.

Disney

Small children and animals
sleep deepest, their eyes
opening slowly as if
through water or wavy glass—
but just a kiss, a tickle
of dust in the palm
of your hand and they disappear.
Peter Pan poised just
for a moment over
the wet lips of the crocodile,
then swam off to rescue
cinnamon-skinned Tiger Lily
before the end of the show.

If Bambi could live
forever he would still have
root-beer eyes, and nibble bark
from a birch. And he would
be both male and female,
chest, breast deeper in fur
each winter, the long
beige body stroked down
to a snowy rump.

It's true, Ichabod Crane
was more lovely
than Brom Bones or any
of the Sleepy Hollow boys.
A single candle held
his shadow up as he wrote in bed.
What I would give to write
all night in that deep blue
notebook, thinking, touching my own
cheek with the blue feather pen.

In Season

"... strawberries ... arrived here, dusty, covered with sand, but in large quantities ... trays fetched, Peter, Daddy, Van Daan, clattering on the stairs ... the loud noises and banging doors positively gave me the jitters. Are we really supposed to be in hiding?"
Anne Frank: The Diary of A Young Girl

It wasn't easy
squeezing strawberries by the fistful
and not squealing when the juice
jumped in your hand.
You had to let all
the pulp drip from your fingers
into the bucket, then
you could lick them.
Out there somewhere
a Dutch family was kneeling
in a field, sniffing the air,
the grubby boy grabbing
fruit from the dirt.
The Grüne Polizei might
have been walking under your window
not knowing how much
you had left to do: stew
strawberries, jar strawberry jam,
wipe sand from the leftovers
and sugar them.

The next week there were potfuls
of peas, too dull
for a teenage girl, you yawned,
as you unzipped each pod,
let the peas slip out,
and skinned the lining
to keep it sweet for cooking.
You sneaked off for a nap,

came back, and there were still
more to wash, split, skin.
You said it made you seasick—
all those pale peas rolling
across spread newspaper
that said the Allies had taken
Caen, Bayeux, Cherbourg.

In August it was over.
The Polizei cracked
your secret wall. The Gestapo
kicked the cupboard door down
and cleaned the place out except
for your notebooks—
they threw them on the floor, here,
there, they left a bootprint
on a page.

You Said,

I will lose you. The dead
are always betrayed.

Your throat packed up
with its jewels,
you turned on the motor
and entered that country
of blue smoke.

I never could love you.
But how my hands ache
from holding
their own bones.

Raking Leaves

for Aunt Grace

White walls, white weather
in the Latham Village Apartments.
Concrete stairs are poured
flat for the small steps
of the old. On your single bed
the starlet's breasts shine up
from a magazine. Smoke snags
in the air, but there's no
bonfire here, only cigarette
breath, and the leaves on this
leaf-print housedress will
never curl.

Ten piles of maple leaves,
ten years. I skipped school
and sneaked through the yard
where you were already
knee-deep in red leaves,
with your red brown hair.
We combed an acre that fall,
smoothed a path away from
the house, then crackled down
on our backs at noon and shared
a six-pack. Barney laughed,
Men's work! You wore his hunting
jacket, and we got them all up
by the first frost.

Who said a woman like you
should live here?
Air conditioning wheezes
across your bedstand, ash trays
full of lipstick butts. I press
my breasts against the sliding window
that seals out spring, summer, and fall.

In Your House, The Museum

Hermitage Museum
Norfolk, Virginia

I can almost see you
lounging in lace, stepping barefoot
over butterfly pegs in the floor
of your favorite room. Never
to tear your skin on a nail,
you'd prop your legs
on this block of pure onyx
and look out at a river in Virginia
through French windows.

Your sixty-year-old son still
sleeps in a roped-off room
where we can't go. But you
are gone, and so is the husband
who was so rich he could have
this house shipped for you,
mahogany beam by beam by crystal
doorknob, across the ocean
to the banks
of your own backyard.

One whole room is a Chinese dynasty
where fine ivory jugs wait
to fill with fingernail parings,
headrests to keep the hair
of the dead in place as they journey
into the afterlife.

This way, says the guide, and points
to the stairs where you waited
for your husband for the last time.
Not a breath
of dust along the banister.

The crowd swirls into place
like a full skirt
on the limestone landing.

Soon she lets us out
on the formal lawn.
Everyone whispers and wind
from the water makes thick
magnolia leaves shuffle slowly
like a sailor's old, soft
deck of cards, killing time.

Spring Cleaning

In the photograph you are twenty-two.
You have stepped out from shadows
into the eye of the camera,
my mother
considering how to smile.

On my bureau you live again,
a girl full of smells
and a dark water.
In my room all spring, you marry.
Children break from you
like bubbles.
A white needled wind
stings the crocus.

Here, Mother.
I give back your cider hair,
hoary wrists and plum belly.
I give back your breasts.

Now it is me.
Lime trees sift their butter.
In the mirror, I am in love with my hips.
You are knocking through the years,
through the steamy showers, saying,
Hurry dear, please come out.

The sun bursts its pod.
I will roll up my shadow.
Coming, Coming. . . .

Medusa

Maybe it was
my tortoise-shell comb that drew
him to me as I pulled it through
waves and waves of my hair,
as I combed my hair right there
in the temple. I watched
Athena's altar through a screen
of sunlight on my hair, and she
watched Neptune tiptoe to the edge
of me, kiss my hair, twist it
around his fingers and slip
it over his shoulders like
a god's robe. But stop. She

stopped us. Stopped my hair
flowing underneath us.
Stopped it forever.
I try to concentrate on braiding,
braiding these thick snakes
down my neck and back.

I smell the salt smell
of a boy. I feel his shadow
sliding by. But I must not
lift my head to look
at him, to sculpt
his whole body.

Insomnia

Father Varden told me it's alright
for children to lie awake thinking.
While my mother cools off on the porch
I wrap up in her quilt and watch summer
reruns. In the hospital scene the little girl's
head is bandaged bald. When the nurses
loosen the gauze, she has no eyes.
My mother comes in and turns it off, lets
a white hole suck the gasping nurses.

But how easily they climb out later.
They hold onto warm dials, their smocks
crackle into our living room. I lie
on the sofa and listen to them rasping
about girls, about summer. They say
Go ahead, close your eyes.
But I don't want to.

Witches' Winter

In 1692 . . . "the girls were in and out of the Reverend Parris household, and probably learning much from Tituba."
The Devil in Massachusetts Marion L. Starkey

In 1706 Ann Putnam publicly begged forgiveness for her role as one of the young accusers in the Salem witch trials.

Tituba touched me.
Her fingertips drew links
in my heartline, counted
the husbands there and whispered,
Not this winter, but soon,
soon. Her hands were hot gold
by the kitchen fire
and each bright card that flashed
through her fingers
had the devil's picture painted
on it, but I looked anyway
and did not stop his features
from melting into her palm,
melting into my body as she
stroked me later and told me
about wicked silks and summer
in some other girl's life.

No longer
did the dried fruit hang
over the mantel. I saw
pale apples and pumpkins get plump
and smooth and bright
as Barbados.
The lug-pole leaned
on the chimney and hung on
to its pot-hooks, pots,
skillets, but I saw them

scalding winter sunlight, and heard them
tinkle and clink until I could hardly
stop myself from dancing just
one forbidden dance.

I began to see how women
in the village really lived,
pricking their babies' necks, rubbing
their own hips until they shrank
down to sleek cat haunches
and scampered away
in the dusk. I saw
the shape of Goody Bishop
over a gentleman's bed, putting
the flicker of her tongue out
in his ear. Goody Cory
was no lady, I saw her
open her bone–lace bodice
and give suck to a snake.

I had to dance
in the courtroom, dance
and fall and cry and try
to make the Magistrate see
how a woman could change
to a yellow bird and perch on that beam
above us, waiting to beat
down at me and bite
my mouth forever.

It would have been better
that way, better not to know
that old snow would blot
the ground and finally disappear,
that there would be no end

to boiling linens for our cold
beds, no number for the stitches
in our samplers that Praise God.
At twenty-six, my skin puckers.
I taste dried blood on my lips.
Better not to have tasted
anything, not to have lived
through the first winter
when Reverend and my father
broke chunks of ice
into my christening bowl, and numbed me
into this life.
                        —

Fasting

My father could eat eggs Sunday morning
because he didn't believe.
He dipped warm bread in the yolk,
and we scraped his plate with our stares
but still had to wait three hours
before Communion. We held our veils
down with bobby pins, and followed
my mother up the winding stairs
to the choir loft. Long pipes
on a wall warmed with music as she sang
by an organ with pedals as big
as the man who played them.
I loved the sun pouring in through
the saints' bright robes, and my mother's
red hair, her long red hair. I saw him touch it—
the organist, where the stairs curve
into the church basement,
but I didn't care. Mass was over.
We were going down there
for sweet rolls, sweet rolls with butter.

My Father's House

I'm eight, waiting outside for the men
to carry away the houses from the yards
that A&P bought up. I see them
plunging their hands into dark
suit pockets, by the ramp that lifts
each house. The open cellars gape
toward our lawn, and Mr. Lyons'
front porch grazes our linden
as the houses roll down Shaker Road.

That spring, the gravel driveway
hissed under the wheels each time
they pulled up in their long cars.
They pressed wide envelopes to their
sides, and filed into our house
to talk to you. We always watched
from the hedge as you walked them
to the edge of the road.
You smiled, balanced your beer can
on the mailbox, and shook your head.

They built the market anyway.
Clipping the strawberry runners, they
raised white walls around our windows.
The workers on the loading dock wiped
their hands and winked, and slabs
of veined beef rode by our kitchen
on pulley and chain and dripped
on the lawn. The summer we moved out
you said you'd rent the house

but never sell. You scoured our smell
from the bedrooms, and knelt to varnish
the floor where the A&P would slide
in their silver cabinets and mount

adding machines in the windows.
I made the monthly rounds with you,
a landlord, grumbling about electric bills,
flicking switches and leaving
each room dark when you left it.

Twenty years later, I'm waiting
for you. Inside the house I see
you set your beer can on someone's desk
where a globe tilts under a lamp
and North America glows.
I'm twenty-eight. I'm eight.
I watch you open your hands
above the world, and spin it.

A Curious Erotic Custom

"From antiquity to the recent past, the Chinese regarded the beauty of the tiny foot as a mark of gentility and refinement. . . . For genteel lovers, the tiny foot provided endless amusement."
Chinese Footbinding: The History Of A Curious Erotic Custom
Howard S. Levy

Somewhere a girl
would scream, a high note
quiver, slide along
her father's spine till
his own voice slurred
with pity for her,
and love.

Her mother pulled
the new toes tight—
white beans planted
against their own
flesh. Soon her spine
curled, her rump
got plump, cunt tight
as she walked
in tiny circles
in the house.

Night
after night the cloth
came off, her bare foot
in a man's hands changed
to a half-moon, water-
chestnut. The other foot
still snug in a red
slipper was a pepper
for him to dream
of tasting.

One lover loved
to see her balance
on the bent-back toes.
To see her in pain
made him thick with grief
so she lay back
and let him kiss her
tender bamboo shoots.

Some lovers loved
to drink the water
after she washed
the bindings, or tongue
the fragrant plum pit
she put by her heel.

One wanted only
to slip his finger
beneath the bandage
to find the tiny
crumbs that were
a lady's secret.
This was love—
to close his eyes
while he nudged each
crevice for sweet
sesame seeds.

Fortune Cookies

Yours

The one across the table
loves you. Remember how
I dangled those curls
of Szechuan Tangerine Chicken
for you to taste.
Burnt, sweet peel, I said.
The kitchen door flashed, hissed
sesame oil while I lured you
across the provinces
from your Double Winter Beef.

Mine

Only through pain can we know
pleasure. But how long
lovers praised the pain
of women with their tongues:
lotus, bamboo shoot,
water-chestnut, he'd say and kiss
her bound foot. I think
of the ache of feet slipped
finally out of high heels behind
double-locked doors. Someone
is to blame, though your mouth
is spicy, your lips as soft
as a woman's lips.

Reasons for Living

Medical studies show that patients who lose their senses of taste and smell often become so depressed that they commit suicide.

Today I ate pieces
of wet cloth for breakfast
but tomorrow maybe sugared
French toast.

Tonight the wine you pour
to cheer me up is just
purple water, but tomorrow
my tongue might be stung

by a crop of grapes.
This cheese might finally
let its smoke loose
at the back of my throat.

If I can be patient
and learn to love
the stubble on strawberries
and not think

they will never
foam in me
on that patch of buds
for sweetness. I remember

melted butter fuming
into my skull, a cave
of dough collapsed
on hot berries, burning

my mouth, I couldn't wait,
but now
if I can wait I might wake up
tomorrow

and stumble into the kitchen
where bags of coffee breathe
violently from the center
of the earth.

I must remember
how many, many mornings
that first whiff bolted
into my brain, and blossomed.